USBORNE SIMPLE READERS

THE
FASTEST

Nicole Irving

Illustrated by Peter Wingham

Edited by Heather Amery

Language Consultant: Betty Root
Reading and Language Information Centre
Reading University, England

This is Pip and Ted with their cat, Nipper.

They love racing around on their bicycles.

They want to know what are the fastest things.

First they go and look at a dog race. The fastest dogs are greyhounds.

Then Pip and Ted watch a horse race. Horses can run a bit faster than greyhounds.

Pip and Ted go to Saudi Arabia to see a camel race.
Nipper soon overtakes all the camels.

In Africa, they watch an ostrich race. Ostriches run
faster than any other birds on earth.

4

If all these animals had a race together, which one would win? Which one runs the fastest?

The dog is faster than the camel. The horse is faster than the dog. But the ostrich is the fastest of all.

Pip and Ted want to find out how fast wild animals can run.

Elephants are big and heavy, but can run fast.

Giraffes have such long legs, they run faster.

Cheetahs can run very fast. But they soon get hot and tired, and have to sit down for a rest.

Zebras can keep running fast for a long time before they get tired.

If all the animals joined in a big race, Pip and Ted would know which is the fastest runner on earth.

A man is running in the race too. But most of the animals can run faster than him.

The kangaroo does not really run. It takes long hops, but can keep up with very fast animals.

The cheetah wins the big race. Cheetahs are the fastest runners in the world.

Pip and Ted go to sea to find the fastest swimmers.
Penguins and many fish swim a lot faster than people.

The fastest fish in the
sea are sailfish.

They can race along faster
than most speedboats.

Killer whales are the fastest whales. They swim after big fish and giant squids to catch them.

Pip and Ted need a car to keep up with the fastest bat in the sky. It can fly very fast.

The fastest insects that fly are dragonflies.

The fastest bats are American bats.

The fastest birds in the sky are swifts.

Many monkeys and apes live in trees. They do not walk, but they swing from branch to branch.

Gibbons are the fastest swingers. Running along the ground, Pip and Ted cannot keep up with them.

Pip and Ted want to know which is the fastest sport in the world.

On a race track, cycling is the fastest sport of all. Only machines with engines can go faster.

If you slide down a mountain covered with snow, you can go very fast.

On sleds, people can go as fast as a fast car.
But on skis, people can go even faster.

Pip and Ted are going to find out which is the fastest sport on water.

Boating is much faster than swimming, even if the boat has no sail or engine.

A yacht is the fastest boat without an engine.
But a good windsurfer can overtake a yacht.

In front of them all is the powerboat. It has a huge
engine and is the fastest boat.

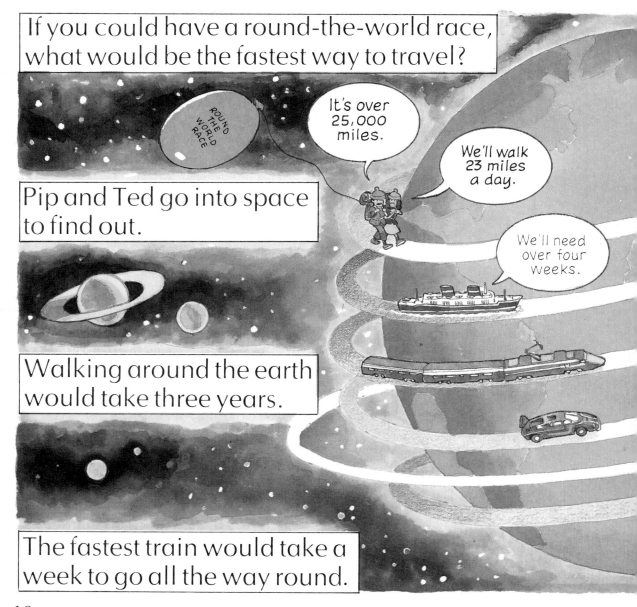

The fastest airliner would only take one day.

The rocket's the fastest.

The car's as fast as the train.

But a rocket would take less than two hours.

19

In America, Pip and Ted watch a tornado.
It is a storm with the fastest winds on earth.

A tornado spins along the ground, smashing
everything in its way.

Pip and Ted go to look
at a volcano.

It is under the sea and
spurts out steam and rocks.

After five days, it has grown into a new island.
Only a volcano can make new land so quickly.

A bamboo is the fastest growing plant. Pip and Ted want to see how much it grows in one day.

In one day, it has grown as tall as an eight year old child.

The fastest growing mushroom is a stinkhorn.
Pip and Ted want to see how fast it grows.

They find one that is just beginning to grow. The
next day, it is fully grown. By evening, it has died.

Pip and Ted have looked at a lot of very fast things.
When they grow up, they want to go very fast.

First published in 1987. Usborne Publishing Ltd, 20 Garrick Street, London WC2E 9BJ, England. © Usborne Publishing Ltd, 1987.

American edition 1987